OSVALDO GOLIJOV
OMARAMOR

FOR SOLO CELLO

HENDON MUSIC

BOOSEY & HAWKES

AN IMAGEM COMPANY

DISTRIBUTED BY

HAL•LEONARD®
CORPORATION

7777 W. BLUEMOUND RD. P.O. BOX 13819 MILWAUKEE, WI 53213

www.boosey.com

www.halleonard.com

Published by Hendon Music, Inc.
a Boosey & Hawkes company
229 West 28th Street, 11th Floor
New York NY 10001

www.boosey.com

© Copyright 2001 Imagem CV
Administered by Hendon Music, Inc., a Boosey & Hawkes company.

ISMN 979-0-051-10748-3

First printing, 2012

Commissioned by Saville Ryan
for the Omar Del Carlo Tanglewood Fellowship

Premiered by Michal Schmidt
at the Painted Bride Arts Center, Philadelphia, PA
November 11, 1991

PROGRAM NOTE

Carlos Gardel, the near-mythical tango singer, was young, handsome, and at the pinnacle of his popularity when the plane that was carrying him to a concert crashed and he died, in 1935. But for all the people who are seated today at the sidewalks in Buenos Aires and listening to Gardel's songs on their radios, that accident is irrelevant because they will tell you, "Today Gardel is singing better than yesterday, and tomorrow he'll sing better than today."

In one of his perennial hits, "My Beloved Buenos Aires," Gardel sings:
> The day I'll see you again,
> My beloved Buenos Aires,
> Oblivion will end,
> There will be no more pain.

Omaramor is a fantasy on "My Beloved Buenos Aires": the cello walks, melancholy at times and rough at others, over the harmonic progression of the song, as if the chords were the streets of the city. In the midst of this wandering the melody of the immortal song is unveiled.

—Osvaldo Golijov

NOTA AL PROGRAMA

Carlos Gardel, figura casi mítica del tango, era joven, apuesto y en 1935 se encontraba en el punto más álgido de su popularidad cuando murió, al estrellarse el avión que lo llevaba a un concierto. Pero para la gente que se sienta a escuchar sus canciones en las veredas de Buenos Aires el accidente es irrelevante. Ellos dirán: "Gardel canta hoy mejor que ayer y
mañana cantará mejor".

En uno de sus éxitos de siempre, "Mi Buenos Aires querido", Gardel canta:

> Mi Buenos Aires querido,
> cuando yo te vuelva a ver,
> no habrá más penas, ni olvido.

Omaramor es una fantasía sobre "Mi Buenos Aires querido": el chelo camina sobre la progresión armónica de la canción, a ratos melancólico y a ratos con dureza, como si los acordes fueran las calles de la ciudad. En medio de este divagar, se revela la melodía de esta canción inmortal.

—Osvaldo Golijov

PROGRAMMHEFT

Carlos Gardel starb im Jahre 1935. Der fast mythische Tangosänger war jung, gut aussehend und auf dem Höhepunkt seiner Popularität angelangt, als das Flugzeug in dem er zu einem Konzert flog abstürzte. Dieser Unfall, jedoch, ist für all jene Leute, die heute am Straßenrand sitzen und Gardel's Lieder aus ihren Radios hören, unirrelevant. Denn sie werden dir sagen: "Heute singt Gardel besser als gestern und morgen wird er besser singen als heute.

In einem seiner ewigen Hits "My Beloved Buenos Aires" singt Gardel:

> Der Tag an dem ich dich wiedersehen werde,
> Mein geliebtes Buenos Aires,
> Wird Vergessenheit enden,
> Wird es keinen Schmerz mehr geben.

Omaramor ist eine Fantasie über "My Beloved Buenos Aires": Manchmal melancholisch, manchmal rau läuft das Cello über die harmonischen Fortschreitungen des Liedes – ganz so, als ob die Akkorde die Straßen der Stadt wären. In der Mitte dieser Wanderung wird die Melodie dieses immerwährenden Liedes vorgestellt.

—*Osvaldo Golijov*

Tempo di tango, ma più mosso e cantabile

f sempre

poch. rubato

stringendo poco a poco

rit.

A tempo, ancora più cantabile

f

dolce — *mp*

Tempo di tango, risoluto

Più pesante   **gradually lifting**

a los fuegos de Saville

Omaramor
for solo cello

Edited by Michal Schmidt

OSVALDO GOLIJOV

*) The C string should be tuned to B♮. The piece is notated at sounding pitch throughout.

ISMN 979-0-051-10748-3

* The low C string should be lowered to Bᵇ (for the entire piece). What should sound is what is written.